Foreword

Mark Bowler

The A835 is one of my all-time favourite roads. Linking bustling Inverness city to the lonely and remote wilds of Assynt within the space of a two hour drive, it never fails to set the pulse racing with anticipation of the adventure ahead. A vast expanse of mountain and moorland, containing hundreds of lochs and lochans, tumbling, rocky burns and rivers, and a coastline as wild as the wild west beckons. Adventure and Assynt go hand-in-hand.

On previous adventures to Assynt I've always found that within minutes of arriving the pace of life calms to a stroll and continues that way for the rest of the trip leaving me with only Ordnance Survey map, compass, tent and fly rod and of course a huge smile on my face.

Assynt is still the same place today as it was many many years ago when I first ventured up there but under the new initiative to promote Assynt as a trout angling destination I can now hire a guide to take me out into the lochs or call the 'Trout Line' to make enquiries and get up to the minute fishing information.

washes through you constantly, like therapeutic balm. Relax, and take in some of the most stunning scenery in Scotland - striking Stac Polly, Suilven's distinctive saddle, and the imposing, seemingly inaccessible Canisp. This is the domain of peat, scree and hidden lochs; the secretive habitat of curlew, ring ouzel and red-throated divers.

The lochs too are all different with some producing a myriad of dark trout of three to the pound on every cast whilst next door you'll catch only bright, fat, yellow-bellied pan fish that fight like dervishes; and then others where you'll be casting over gin clear water that holds trout the size of small dogs!

Big lochs such as Assynt, Fionn, Veyatie and Sionascaig all have their classic leviathan trout fishing stories to tell but there are also masses of smaller lochs within the parish that can produce fish well beyond the size you would think were in them. So with all that going on, where on earth does the holidaying angler start? Right here. How handy it is for Cathel Macleod to share this book with us - a book so full of juicy angling secrets I simply can't wait until I next turn onto the A835 again. And again.

Mark Bowler is editor of Fly Fishing and Fly Tying magazine.

Ardvreck Castle, Loch Assynt

1

Author's Preface
Cathel MacLeod

From Suilven with Cam Loch in the distance

In Assynt there are hundreds of hill lochs most of which contain trout of one description or another; little, large, fat, thin, free taking, dour, and so on, they are all here. Where does one begin? Which lochs should I try? Where are the best fish? What about beginners? Are there any salmon? The questions are as legion as the answers required. Trying to decide on an angling venue in the absence of proper information is the classic 'fisherman's nightmare' especially when looking at a map displaying countless lochs and rivers. With that scenario in mind, I have attempted to provide a few of the answers in this booklet and I hope that it will be a helpful and useful guide for anyone who visits Assynt on a fishing holiday.

It would be impossible to include all the lochs and rivers along with relative data in a publication of this nature, so I have chosen some of the best with large crafty trout that are difficult to entice, others with a variety of less cunning fish, and a handful with lots of smaller brownies that are easier to catch, suitable for beginners or anybody else seeking a good day's sport. There is something here for everyone.

All the information contained within is based on my own fishing experience over the past fifty years, along with some gleaned by me from others during that time. Any minor inaccuracies in descriptions of lochs or rivers is down to fading memories on my part, but the detail of how to get there in each case is one hundred per cent correct. All names and grid references are taken from Ordnance Survey Landranger Map Sheet No 15 /1:50,000. The grid reference for each loch indicates somewhere about its centre, just to make sure that it will not be missed by inaccurate navigation.

Good luck, and may the bends in your fishing rod be as many as those in the road to Assynt.

Contents

Map Use

Anglers MUST carry a map with them and preferably a compass also when fishing in the area due to the terrain and walking that is often required to reach some of the outlying lochs. All grid references referred to in this booklet relate to Sheet No 15 Ordnance Survey Landranger Series 1:50 000 Scale which can be purchased in a number of local outlets including the Tourist Information Centre in Lochinver. If you're not familiar with maps or how to navigate using them please ask for advice at the Tourist Information Centre in Lochinver.

Permits, Boats and Angling Enquiries

All lochs and rivers mentioned within this booklet are covered by a Government Protection Order, meaning that it is a legal requirement for a permit to be purchased in order to fish in the area. For all angling enquires including the purchasing of permits and booking of boats contact the Tourist Information Centre on 01571 844497 during 9am to 5pm.

Fly fishing is generally what it's about in Assynt and below are some guidelines to help you bring the right gear when you come to the area.

RODS

Dry fly fishing is popular in Assynt and there's nothing more intimate than crawling along the margins of a loch on a calm day or evening casting small dries on a 3 or 4 weight rod to cruising trout. However the wind is well known in this area too and a 15ft+ dapping rod used from a boat in a wave can often bring up the best fish of the day to a big danced fly. If you're boating and you're not on for dapping or it's not windy enough you would do well to use a rod between 11-12ft in length. It's true that wild trout respond well to flies near or on the surface and a rod of this length allows you much more control of your flies as you bring them to the surface and dibble them in the top layers of the water. It is a very successful method and often out-fishes the shorter rod from the boat.

Needless to say a 9-10ft #5-7 weight rod is a standard piece of equipment today for most fly fishing anglers and this would be the rod of choice if only one rod was brought to cover a wide variety of situations.

LINES & REELS

Sooner or later it's likely that you will connect with a steam train of a trout that will test your gear to the limit, saying nothing of your nerves, so make sure you attach at least 75 yards of backing to your flyline and have a reel with an effective drag system. 5 or 6lb monofilament tippet is fine as the fish are not that shy but I suspect that fine diameter fluorocarbon will attract more fish over time, but it should be stiff enough so as not to tangle whenever the wind blows. Again long tippet lengths may assist in calmer conditions but I have seen many anglers with leaders ranging from 6ft to 9ft pulling in basket loads of fish from these lochs so don't feel you have to get all technical in order to enjoy your fishing because you don't!

TACTICS

Traditional Scottish wet fly has been the most widely used technique in this part of the world since most of us can remember. And they are traditional because essentially, they work, and work very well. Names like Bibio, Black Pennell, Soldier Palmer, Blue Zulu, Wickhams Fancy, Kate McLaren, Claret Bumble, Goat's Toe, Octopus, Invicta/Silver Invicta, Green Peter and a host of others have stood the test of time on wild trout so don't be afraid to use them if you want to catch fish! Dry fly is also widely used in the area to great effect and can often be the taker of the best fish of the day! In addition to traditional wet and dry fly there are exciting opportunities for nymph and buzzer fishing, both of which have been proved in recent years to be very effective and often account for bigger fish.

CLOTHING

The sentiment regarding clothing is 'be prepared' as the weather can change from warm and sunny to rain and dropping temperatures without much notice. In order to reach many of the lochs in this booklet a walk of some description is required, so bring a pair of walking boots. You can keep them on all day and just cast from the bank or change into waders on arrival at the loch and carry the boots in your day pack until heading home again. Although not necessary, a pair of lightweight chest or thigh waders can be advantageous on some lochs in helping you to cover more water.

A hat is definitely recommended – it can protect your face from harmful sun rays, keep your head warm on cold days and as importantly, protect you from any errant casts you, or somebody else might make! A waterproof jacket is essential for every trip away from the road. Something lightweight and foldable is ideal but you should never head into the hills without one as it will help keep your body temperature up if cold and wet conditions suddenly descend.

Take a small rucksack to carry any waders, spare clothing, food and drink and your map in during the day. The pack can easily be worn whilst fishing and in my experience has never restricted my casting at all. Oh yes, and don't forget to take a 'midge net'. If the wind drops to nothing whilst during warm conditions this head net will be the only thing to protect you from the enthusiastic attention of this well known little insect!

For all your clothing and tackle needs call or visit The Lochinver Chandlery in the village by the harbour (01571 844 398).

4

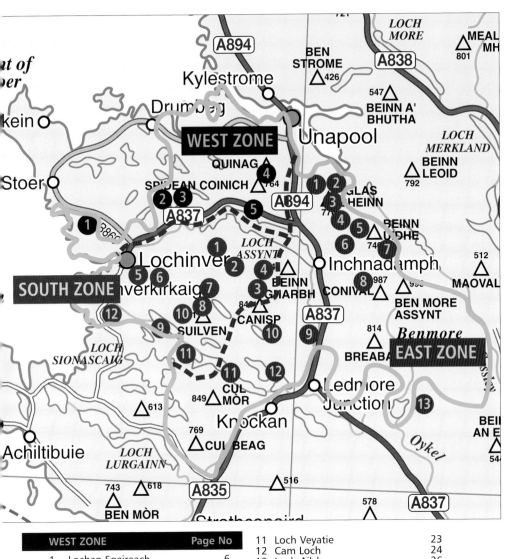

Lochan Sgeireach

(1)

Grid Reference 15/072255

WALK: EASY 🏃🏃

Approximate Time:	10 minutes
Distance:	350 metres
How to get there:	To get to Lochan Sgeireach park at the viewpoint beside the B869 road about 4kms north of Lochinver and from there walk due west up the nearby gully for about 200 metres, climbing on to the low ridge immediately to the south. Once on top of the ridge, carry on west for another 150 metres or so and the loch is just a short distance ahead and below. It should only take 10 minutes to get there from the road.

This small, narrow loch is the water supply for Achmelvich village. It is deep all round its perimeter and is home to some very large brown trout. Being virtually weed free with very clear water, the resident fish are shy and difficult to tempt so visitors often come away empty-handed. Stocked occasionally with limited numbers of indigenous unfed fry, the fish grow on quickly, feeding hard on the large quantities of natural food items found in the loch. Trout caught here are usually large and in recent times fish up to 7½lbs have been taken with several others around the 5-6lb mark landed.

Not a loch for the whole day due to its relatively small size, but its ease of access makes for a perfect place to visit for a couple of hours in the afternoon or evening with the rather remote chance of catching a specimen trout.

If anything, the loch fishes best in winds from a westerly or easterly direction. Winds from other directions tend to swirl all over the place, making it nigh on impossible to cast with any confidence and in this situation anglers would be well advised to return at another time. Fishing is easy round most of the loch though wading is not possible due to the depth of the water close to the bank.

Conservation is the prolonged existence of the trout in these small wild waters so please restrict the number of fish retained, if any.

1lb 15oz trout from Loch Sgeireach

Loch Beannach

2

WALK: EASY 👥

Approximate Time:	25 minutes
Distance:	1km
How to get there:	Access is gained from the same starting point as that for Loch an Ruighein (page 8). Once en route, walk along the outside of the deer fence to the point where it turns sharp right. Here head due north up the short steep slope in front which is pretty well defined by foot erosion. On reaching the top, Beannach can be seen a few hundred yards further on. Gradually move away from the fence and continue down to the loch where the boats can be easily found. It is about 1km from the road and no more than an easy 25 minute walk.
Boats available:	Two boats are available, located at **Grid Reference 15/141262**.

A beautiful and sprawling loch, festooned with tree-covered islands, Beannach is home not only to a vast population of wild brown trout, but also arctic char and a few salmon and sea trout although neither of the latter have been reported caught in recent years.

A great day's sport is what it's all about on Beannach. The average isn't large at less than 8ozs but there are plenty much bigger than that there. With lots of free taking trout, the pleasure of continuously catching fish on a lovely summer's day is hard to beat for enjoyment. As one might expect, bank fishing sometimes produces very good baskets and they can be caught everywhere around the countless bays and promontories. Having said that, boat fishing is better and recommended as it offers the ability to fish all around the many islands found in the eastern part where there is good feeding and shelter for the fish. On this very convoluted water boats give the advantage to cover a greater area and move more freely over the loch. Beannach can be fished in winds from all directions, but west or southerlies are best.

Loch Beanach

70 to 80 fish for the boat can be taken here in a day, with a range of sizes making up the basket. In June when the Mayfly are hatching the water can literally 'boil' with, hungry, feeding fish, so it is the right time to cast a well presented fly over their heads.

Loch an Ruighein ③

Grid Reference 15/155268   **WALK: MODERATE** 🚶🚶

Approximate Time:	45 minutes
Distance:	2km
How to get there:	Park in the small tarred parking area adjacent to the A837 road approximately 5kms east of Lochinver at **Grid Reference 15/144254**. A gap in the roadside crash barrier signifies the right place. By foot, head through the opening in what remains of an old stock fence, and follow the grassy track for about 50 metres. Cross over the ditch and go east up around the little hillock in front. Follow this route through the 'kissing' gate in the deer fence some 200 yards further on. Travel northeast through the obvious valley, following the marker poles, which lead to the old, ruined Sheilings. Keep heading north skirting the first smaller loch to the right (east), and Loch an Ruighein will be reached quite quickly a few hundred metres ahead. It shouldn't take any more than 45 minutes from the road to the loch, and the route is quite easy.
Boat available:	A boat is available, located at **Grid Reference 15/155266**.

Known as the Sheiling Loch, this small water contains good numbers of lovely, silvery brownies that commonly average between 8-10ozs although fish over 1lb are not uncommon. Trout can be caught all over the loch, but the area around the islands is very good. It is generally weed free, and fishes well from the bank in a southerly, easterly or westerly breeze. It is a strange phenomena though that for some reason, historically, much better fish have been caught fishing from the boat, same being located at **Grid Reference 15/155266**.

Although Ruighein is the better loch it is well worthwhile having a cast on the first loch on your way back where the fish are hard fighting and average 8-12ozs. It is quite weedy but some good trout up to around the one pound mark can be caught in the clear areas.

Fishing the River Kirkaig out of Fionn Loch

Lochan Bealach Cornaidh ④

Grid Reference 15/208282　　　　**WALK: MODERATE** 🚶🚶

Approximate Time:	50 minutes
Distance:	2.5km
How to get there:	Lochan Bealach Cornaidh separates the northern peak from the eastern ridge of Quinag, another of Assynt's classic mountains. Named after the bealach where it is located, this beautiful little loch lies tucked away on the valley floor. It takes about 50 minutes to get there on foot, with access commencing from the A894 road about 3kms to the north of Skiag Bridge. Leave the car in the old quarry by the east side of the road, cross the wooden bridge, and walk west on the stalkers footpath towards the mountain. The track, which goes on for a kilometre or so eventually peters out as the steeper ground approaches. Carry on, as far again, in the same direction up the corrie to the waterside.

Some lovely trout inhabit Lochan Bealach Cornaidh. The average fish are silvery in colour with black spots and weigh around 12ozs, however fish between 2 and 3lbs are taken from time to time and it has produced fish up to 5lbs in past years, so cast carefully from its shores! Although sometimes on the dour side, fish are caught all round the loch. They tend to congregate in the better daytime habitat off the deeper edge at the foot of the mountain so pay particular attention to that part. The water is very clear so take care not to spook fish when approaching the edge and walking along the bank.

The north side and the western end are both shallow and wading above the knee is necessary in order to cover fish properly. The rest of the loch can easily be fished from the bank. It is pretty weed free with only small patches appearing here and there. A northerly or easterly wind produces the best conditions.

On the way home, try the little, seemingly insignificant tarns to the north of the footpath. They can sometimes surprise with a very fine fish!

2lb 10oz trout from Loch Bealach Cornaidh

9

Loch Assynt

⑤

Grid Reference 15/207248

WALK: EASY 🚶🚶

Approximate Time:	n/a
Distance:	Roadside
How to get there:	Access is gained to the mid boat from the lay-by at the south side of the A837 road, which is immediately adjacent to where the boat is moored, with the Assynt Head boat being located via the rough road leading down to the little church at Inchnadamph, heading west off the main A837. Drive past the church, through the unlocked gate near the loch side and the boat will be seen there on a running mooring.
Boats available:	There are two boats available, located at mid-Assynt **Grid Reference 15/202260** and at Assynt Head (east end), **Grid Reference 15/248221.**

Loch Assynt is a vast and deep expanse of water dropping to over 80 metres in some parts. About 8kms long by 1.5kms broad at its widest point, it is the largest loch in the parish and dominates the drive from Inchnadamph much of the way to Little Assynt along the A837 road. Brown trout, ferox, arctic char, salmon and sea trout all inhabit this place and add their own character to an enigmatic water. Although brown trout only average somewhere about 8ozs there is a huge head of fish here and consequently quite a lot of fish in the 1-2lb bracket are present and many are caught each year with some in considerable excess of this weight. A 14lb trout was taken recently on opening day so always be prepared for the chance of a real 'lunker' having a go at your flies! As usual, the best fly fishing is found around the edges, being particularly relevant here because of the rapid fall off to the deeps quite close inshore. This rule of thumb is obviously less relevant to those fishing for ferox where many of the leviathans are taken from the deeper water.

The most productive areas from the boat are as follows:-

At Assynt Head (the eastern end of the loch) fish all round where the River Loanan enters the loch continuing along the northern shoreline through Castle Bay, and the mouth of the Calda Burn just to the east of Ardvreck Castle as this area has a reputation for producing good fish. Watch out for grilse rock in the middle of the bay, where the water is shallow. At low levels the rock is exposed, but in high water it is just sub-surface and can take you by surprise. The bay to the west of the castle should also be fished and it is worth keeping your flies on the surface from there along to the Skiag burn and the pulpit rock which protrudes from the loch a little further on. The area around the burn and rock is shallow, and the fish tend to congregate there. The next 2kms are generally unproductive, unless trolling further out, but concentrate from mid Assynt all the way west to the sluice gates as the myriad of bays and headlands found along this stretch all hold fish.

At the southern side, fish from the entry of the River Loanan west for about 1.5kms through an area noted for its many salmon lies, to salmon point. Look out for the 'Lemon Tree', which bears unusual fruit and marks one of the most prolific salmon areas on the loch. Both salmon point and the next headland to the west are good lies and well worth a cast from the bank. Spend some time in the long bay to the west of the second headland as some good trout have been caught here with the added advantage that you will be covering salmon at the same time! From there west to Shepherd's Bay is good for trolling. Make sure to fish Shepherd's Bay and its neighbour Weaver's Bay thoroughly, especially around the burn mouths as excellent quality fish are often taken from there. Cast in amongst all the skerries in the eastern side of Weaver's bay, principally between Eilean Assynt and the landward shore to cover the good trout that feed on molluscs in the shallower water around the rocks. Deep water round the headland of Rubh'an Alt-toir directly to the west of Weaver's Bay doesn't produce a lot of fish, but after that the southern shore to the sluice gates is all

worth fishing with the added interest of very good trout and salmon lies near the sluices. For no good reason the west end gets a lot less attention, but it can be equally productive for all species, as the rest of this vast expanse of water.

Plugging the safety theme, this place can be really dangerous in high winds from any direction, but chiefly in easterlies or westerlies, which whip up huge breaking waves, capable of overcoming the boat. People have lost their lives here before in those conditions, so please do not become another statistic. Take care at all times.

Please note that there is no Sunday fishing allowed.

Loch Assynt

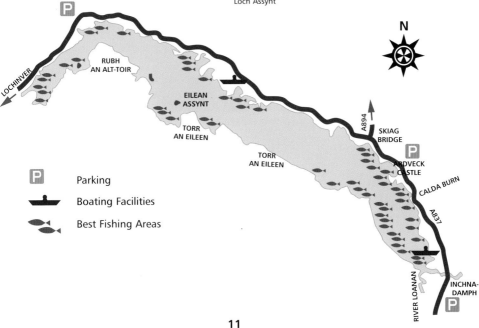

RUBH
AN ALT-TOIR

LOCHINVER

EILEAN
ASSYNT

TORR
AN EILEEN

TORR
AN EILEEN

SKIAG
BRIDGE

ARDVECK
CASTLE

CALDA BURN

A894

A837

N

Parking

Boating Facilities

Best Fishing Areas

RIVER LOANAN

INCHNA-
DAMPH

Loch a Choire Dheirg (Red Corrie) ①

Grid Reference 15/253273   WALK: MODERATE 🚶🚶

Approximate Time:	1 hour
Distance:	1.5kms
How to get there:	Turn north onto the A894 at Skiag Bridge on Loch Assynt and drive up the hill for about 4kms where a single metal post on the east side of the road locates the parking area. From here follow the footpath for about 400 metres before heading southeast up the hillside into the lower part of the Red Corrie. Carry on up the corrie until you arrive at the loch. The total distance from the road is just over 1.5kms, but the ground is steep, so allow about 1hr for the walk in.

Known locally by its English translation, the 'Red Corrie Loch' is located in a basin on the northern slopes of Glas Bheinn. A small, circular hill loch, shielded and surrounded on three sides by very steep, high ground, it fishes best in northwest wind, to which it is exposed without much interference from the surrounding terrain.

The trout here are fairly plentiful and of excellent quality, averaging around 1lb in weight, with quite a few up to and exceeding 2lbs. The crystal clear water means they 'spook' easily making them difficult to tempt so take care when approaching and moving along the bank. Beautiful brownies can be taken all round the loch, there being no particular hot spots, so keep close observation on your flies all the time. Big 'bags' are unlikely, but the challenge, along with the added bonus of walking amongst spectacular surroundings, makes this a memorable trip and additionally one which can be combined with a visit to neighbouring Green Corrie Loch over the ridge, described elsewhere in this booklet.

A beautifully marked fish from Loch a Choire Dheirg

Un-named Loch (Little Green) ②

Grid Reference 15/264275   WALK: MODERATE 🏃🏃

Approximate Time: 1 hour 30 minutes
Distance: 3.5kms
How to get there: To get there, park by the A894 road about 4kms north of Skiag Bridge. A single metal post at the north side of the road indicates the parking area. From this point follow the footpath along the southern shore of Loch na Gainmhich, up into Bealach a' Bhuirich. Carry on via the path as it takes you on uphill and alongside Loch Bealach a' Bhuirich. Attain the highest point on the path just beyond the eastern end of the latter, and leave the track heading due south over the undulating ground towards the eastern escarpment of Glas Bheinn. 'Little Green' can be fiddly to chance upon, but not much over 15 minutes from the track should bring you to it.

Those of us who fish here from time to time have imposed the name 'Little Green' on this lochan for identification purposes only. As the name suggests, it is a very small water, and many people omit to cast a fly here, as they walk hurriedly by with great expectations of better things ahead. Its name derives from the nearby Green Corrie Loch, which is talked about elsewhere in this booklet.

It is well worth stopping and casting over Little Green's water though as it holds a good population of excellent quality trout. The fish average in excess of 1lb and when the Mayfly are hatching here, the whole surface can often boil with feasting red and black spotted brownies. It is not surprising then that with an average like this there are many fish landed between 1½- 2½lbs in weight with a superb fish several times that weight being caught there in recent years.

Like all clear water lochs, much time, skill and patience, is required to entice one of those fish with an artificial fly, but it can be done, given good conditions.

Situated on a plateau just to the north of the Green Corrie Loch itself this water fishes well in most winds other than from the south or south west being sheltered from those by the mountain of Glas Bheinn. Apart from in the south-western bay and occasionally along the northwest shore, the loch is weed free and easily fished from the bank without need for wading. Cast carefully all round giving particular attention to the area near the big rock on the west shore and amongst the rocky outcrops in the water on the north side. The southern shore is all good but pay particular attention where the burn comes in.

Be careful in misty or foggy conditions as one can easily get lost with the ground being featureless and similar all around. Taking a correct compass bearing just before leaving the track is never bad practice and especially so in the above circumstances. Total distance from the road to the water's edge is about 3.5kms, with the last 500 metres over rough hill ground. There is a fair bit of steep ascent on the footpath, which itself is quite uneven in parts, thus allow about 1.5 hours to comfortably reach the loch from the road.

Be mindful of fish preservation on this very small tarn, and return as many as possible to the water please.

Lochan a Choire Ghuirm (Green Corrie Loch) ③

Grid Reference 15/262267   WALK: MODERATE 🚶🚶

Approximate Time:	1 hour 45 minutes
Distance:	5kms
How to get there:	By taking the route to 'Little Green' (page 13), and then following the in-flow burn upstream on its right hand side, you will come to Choire Ghuirm after approximately 0.5kms and about 15 minutes walking time. The whole journey from the road to Green Corrie Loch should be easily accomplished in 1 hour 45 minutes or less.

This loch is set on the floor of the Green Corrie amidst some of the finest scenery in the area. Glas Bheinn towers like a bodyguard over its southern and western shores, and the view from here north to the distant Reay Country, and eastwards to the flatter areas of central Sutherland, is truly awe-inspiring. In addition to its setting though, this loch attracts fishers for another good reason, which is simply the size and quality of its residents. The walk in, or up to the loch, which sits at 550 metres above the sea, will certainly exercise the legs, heart and lungs, whilst one makes all haste to access the place, without wasting too much fishing time en-route.

A sparkling clear water covering an area of around 4 hectares which in most parts is only 2 metres or so deep, it hosts some of the finest wild brown trout in Assynt. Most of the fish exceed 1½lbs in weight but each season several trout in the 3-5lb class are caught. They are splendid specimens. Deep bodied, with small heads, big tails and a silvery/green colouring on their flanks, which makes them almost translucent in appearance. When seen in the water, their camouflage is so well suited to their surroundings that they become almost invisible to the human eye.

The fish do not give themselves up easily. Patience and stealth are required to capture an inhabitant from here and blank days are common enough. Fishing is easy from the bank when the wind blows steadily from the north, northwest or east, but it can be a testing experience if arriving from any other direction as it swirls around playing havoc with one's casting. On this note, and in those circumstances, it is wise to wear protective eyeglasses and a hat as both can help to avoid nasty and painful accidents.

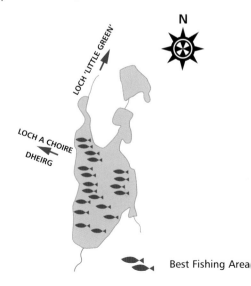

Best Fishing Area

Frequently, in the right conditions, large trout can be seen moving on the surface, with the odd one swirling to a hatching fly, and others just leisurely cruising around feeding on whatever insects are available. Occasionally considerable numbers are observed, rising all over the place, which makes for extremely stimulating and exciting fishing. It is wise not to expect this sort of activity though, as not seeing anything all day can be just as typical.

Fish right round the loch as success can come from anywhere, skirting the southern end, which is very shallow. Anywhere else in the loch is good, but the following spots are worth paying particular attention to. Carefully fish the promontory at the northern end as many of the best fish have been taken here. Carry on along the western shore making sure to spend some time fishing by the large stone that protrudes out of the water, as trout are often seen feeding there. Try along the rocky eastern shoreline and around the little island. Lots of trout seem to gather by this shore, so keep your eyes and your flies on the water. Both wet fly and nymph will take fish but it is the dry fly that seems to attract these great fish more than anything else, so cast it, leave it, and see what happens!

There are two or three other little tarns in the vicinity of the main loch, but only the latter contains fish.

Conservation is the lifeblood of these small wild waters so please help them survive by respecting the number of fish, if any that are kept.

Lochan a Choire Ghuirm

Loch Bealach na h-Uidhe ④

Grid Reference 15/264256 **WALK: MODERATE** 🚶🚶

Approximate Time: 1 hour 50 minutes
Distance: 6kms
How to get there: Leave the car in the car park just off the A837 road at the Inchnadamph Hotel at **Grid Reference 15/254217**. Walk along the road over the River Traligill and immediately turn right (east) onto an un-tarred car track following it for approximately 800 metres before taking the path up the hillside to the northeast. Follow this route up and around Cnoc an Droighinn keeping straight on where the path splits at the small shelter hut and continue north towards Loch Fleodach Coire following the little cairns of stones laid by walkers where the path is less obvious. Pass by Loch Fleodach Coire using the rather indistinct path that touches its western shoreline, continuing uphill, due north, for some 300 metres. Try and keep to this very indefinite path as it heads northwest up and along the side of Beinn Uidhe. Very soon the loch is seen about 400 metres away over to the left in the bed of the corrie. Don't be fooled by following the burn that drains Loch Bealach na h-Uidhe into Loch Fleodach Coire. Although it is a more direct route it is exceedingly rough underfoot and makes for very slow progress.

A true hill loch, tucked 530 metres up the mountain in a little corrie. Some 1.5 hours from the road this loch, according to many, is what trout fishing in Assynt is all about. Although relatively small, it is not one to pass by as the trout here are of truly excellent quality and size. They average 1-1½lbs with fish up to 2½lbs not being uncommon as part of the bag. Big baskets are not what its about here but in good conditions having a few of these beautiful trout come to the fly over as many hours is quite usual. Unlike many other small lochs, this one is weed free and fishes best in an easterly or southeasterly wind being sheltered by the surrounding mountains from most other directions. Wading is nigh impossible as the water is quite deep close in. Fish are taken all round the loch with perhaps the northeastern shoreline being marginally better. It is a fact that bigger fish up to and over 3lbs come into the edges and cruise in the margins. To cast at and catch one of those magnificent specimens in surroundings like this is a humbling, but wonderful experience indeed, for any trout fisher.

Please be conservation minded when fishing small, comparatively productive waters, like this. Think of the future, so be prudent about retaining fish.

Allow at least one and three-quarter hours to get there from the car park. It is pretty much uphill all the way so stop now and again to catch breath, and admire the view.

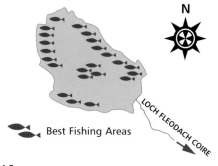

N

Best Fishing Areas

LOCH FLEODACH COIRE

Loch Fleodach Coire ⑤

Grid Reference 15/274248

WALK: MODERATE 🚶🚶

Approximate Time:	1 hour 20 minutes
Distance:	5kms
How to get there:	To get to Loch Fleodach Coire, follow exactly the same directions as described for getting to Loch Bealach na h-Uidhe (page 16), stopping off at the appropriate spot. The journey from the road at Inchnadamph to the loch takes about an hour and twenty minutes.

An interesting trout loch set in the Fleodach Coire basin, at the foot of Beinn Uidhe, about 400 metres above sea level. Although shown on the Ordnance Survey map as a single loch, it is in fact two completely separate waters, the eastern part being separated from the west by a little stream. The western and larger part of the loch holds trout of a standard averaging 8ozs, with fish ranging from very small up to 1½lbs and occasionally over. It can be fished all round with the exception of the south-western bay which is pretty well overgrown with weed and un-fishable. The northern shore tends to produce better results and sometimes good fish are taken where the burn enters the loch at its western end. Wading is not necessary, although along the western shore it could be advantageous as the water is shallow there for quite a way out from the edge. The fish take freely and a nice basket can be had from this loch.

The smaller eastern part (separate loch) has fish that are of pretty identical size. It is clear of weed and can be fished all round, wading not being necessary.

Loch Bealach na h-Uidhe in the foreground with Fleodach Coire off to the left and Fiddle Loch central in the distance

Un-named Loch (Fiddle Loch) ⑥

Grid Reference 15/270242   WALK: MODERATE 👫

Approximate Time:	1 hour 15 minutes
Distance:	4kms
How to get there:	Refer to Loch Bealach na h-Uidhe (page 16) for initial directions. Getting to this one involves a 50m drop from the Fleodach Coire path down, and then 50m back up, a steep hillside. Because of this the Fiddle loch, although well worth a cast, is not fished all that often. Access is gained by heading north for several hundred metres from the shelter hut that sits at the junction of the two marked paths and then leaving the track when the loch comes into view in the valley immediately below. There is no footpath and the hillside can sometimes be wet so take care when descending down to the water's edge. From the road at Inchnadamph to the loch should take no more than one and a quarter hours or thereby.

The Fiddle Loch, so called locally due to its violin like shape, is unnamed on the Ordnance Survey map. The fish vary in weight from little to large, with an average of just under 8ozs. In recent years several accounts of big trout jumping in the loch have been related, although fish of this nature have yet to be caught there to confirm the stories. Sitting in a steep sided valley the loch is part of the main drainage system for the Fleodach Coire tarns that lie some 50m vertically higher to the north east. Fiddle fishes best in a stiff westerly breeze. As the season progresses a fair bit of weed growth occurs but there is still plenty of clear water to cast a line on. There is no need to wade as all of the good areas can be covered from the bank.

Loch Bealach a Mhadaidh from the West

18

Loch Bealach a' Mhadaidh ⑦

Grid Reference 15/310232

WALK: TESTING 𝕏𝕏

Approximate Time:	2.5 hours
Distance:	9kms
How to get there:	The most direct access to this place is by exactly the same way as to Loch Fleodach Coire. On reaching the path junction at the little shelter hut, take the track to the right that descends briefly but gently down to the valley floor, and follow same towards the steep face ahead. The track soon becomes very indistinct, and as it ascends, will probably be lost altogether. Make for Loch na Cuaran, which is a crucial 'landmark' in any event, particularly so if the necessity arises to navigate by map and compass. By-pass the loch via its southwestern side, which is less steep. Progress to the lowest point, on the six hundred and ten metre contour, in the coll that separates Mullach an Leathaid Riabhaich from the neighbouring un-named precipitous, southerly ascending ridge. When the desired position in the coll is reached continue due east. The glen ahead drops very abruptly, and the loch will come quickly into view, a long way below and a shade to the southeast on the corrie floor. An especially sharp drop down is met for most of the way to the loch, so visually choose the best route of descent. Allow in the region of two and a half hours for the whole trek and just a little less for the return journey.

The trip to Loch Bealach a' Mhadaidh is not for the unfit, or faint-hearted. Tucked away in a corrie at the eastern end of Mullach an Leathaid Riabhaich, just short of the three hundred and fifty metre contour, a degree or two of planning is required in order to enjoy a day out there. About nine kilometres from the car park at Inchnadamph, with a hike uphill to a height of around six hundred metres, before dropping down again on the side of a rather precipitous glen, a while is taken to reach it.

A very exciting location to fly-fish; there are all sizes of trout in this water. Like many of the other lochs in Assynt the trout average just around half to three-quarters of a pound on a good day, but reports of numerous specimens in the two to three pound class have been made in recent times, with one of the best bags being a catch of a dozen or so fish up to and including a four pounder taken in a single day. In contradiction, of course, there are other reports of disappointment, when the catches have not been up to expectations.

A reasonably weed free place, which can be fished right round from the edge, the south-western side is steep, and the whole loch is very sheltered from all winds except easterlies. Fish are to be found right around this interesting water so miss no part out. Salmon can, and do, migrate there via the River Cassley system, although it would be considered a stroke of luck to catch one. Such a remote location does not endear this tarn to the average fisherman, and few anglers visit in any year; therefore reports on catches are sparse.

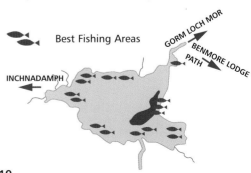

Best Fishing Areas

Loch Mhoalach-coire (Gillaroo Loch) 8

Grid Reference 15/277195 WALK: MODERATE 秋

Approximate Time:	1 hour 15 minutes
Distance:	3.5kms
How to get there:	Vehicles should be left in the public parking area near the Inchnadamph Hotel. From there take the rough road by the north side of the Traligill Burn, and follow it to Glen Bain house. Follow this footpath into the lower part of Gleann Dubh, and just beyond the small plantation of mature fir trees where the track divides, turn right across the Traligill Burn, following the trail up to the loch ahead. The total distance from the road to the loch is about 3.5kms, and walking time is around 1 hour 15 minutes.

The Gillaroo Loch is so called due to a particular type of trout that historically populated the loch. Gillaroo trout have their origins in Northern Ireland, being well known in Lough Melvin. They are different in that their almost exclusive diet of molluscs and crustaceans gives them a very recognisable deep body shape, unlike a 'standard' brown trout. The Gillaroo trout have long gone it seems, but have left a hard fighting population of 'normal' fish that average 8-10ozs in weight with a few much larger specimens occasionally caught. Apart from the superb sport that they provide, today's trout are beautifully pink fleshed and as such are a real treat on the table.

Loch Mhoalach-coire is located south of the Traligill River on the east side of Creagan Breaca in relatively open country, some 270 metres above sea level. A small water of around 8 hectares, it sits on a bed of Durness limestone, and consequently has an abundance of freshwater shrimp for the trout to gorge on. It is not a very deep loch and can be fished from the bank all round although it suffers a bit from weed growth as the season progresses. On a slightly negative note, unlike most places in Assynt, there are no other lochs anywhere in the vicinity to take in whilst you are there. However it is still well worth visiting with the walk up and back being delightful.

Loch Awe

Grid Reference 15/245154

⑨

WALK: EASY 🚶🚶

Approximate Time:	n/a
Distance:	Roadside
How to get there:	The loch is located about 6kms south of Inchnadamph on the A837. Leave your car in the parking area on the east side of the A837 road near the loch.
Boat available:	The boat anchorage at **Grid Reference 15/248157** is easily seen from here and simply walk down the gentle slope to the boat.

Loch Awe is a charming, picturesque, roadside loch, dotted with tree-covered islands. Just over 1km in length by about 0.5km in breadth, with an average depth of about 2 metres, it holds a remarkable stock of wild brown trout. The majority of fish are around the 8oz mark but there are good numbers up to 1½lbs present, with a few bigger ones thrown in. A very popular place with anglers, because of its size, closeness to the road and quality of its fish. During June the loch experiences huge Mayfly hatches and this is a good time to fish it as the trout often pursue them in feeding frenzies which can provide some very exciting fishing. Throughout the season, some salmon make it up the River Loanan from Loch Assynt, however very few are ever caught.

Only boat fishing is allowed here, and to respect local tradition Sunday fishing is not permitted. Fish can be caught all over this shallow water but areas around the islands should be given

particular attention with south or westerly winds giving the best of it. As the season progresses a lot of the surface becomes affected by weed, but there are still plenty of clear areas to fish. This is one of the better lochs in the district and should be on every visiting angler's hit list.

Take care when rowing the boat, and particularly so if using an outboard motor. The southern end, at a point some 250 metres south of the boat anchorage, is separated from the northern end by a shallow, narrow, rocky bar, extending sub-surface from one side of the loch to the other. It is well known as an easy place to go aground so do not panic if it happens to you. In high water the rocks go un-noticed, but at lower levels some sort of collision is just about inevitable. Be aware that this hazard exists, and if it's of any comfort, nobody has come to grief there yet!

N

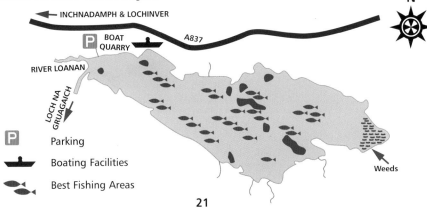

⬅ INCHNADAMPH & LOCHINVER

🅿 **BOAT QUARRY** ⛵ A837

RIVER LOANAN

LOCH NA GRUAGAICH

🅿 Parking

⛵ Boating Facilities

🐟 Best Fishing Areas

Weeds

21

Lochan Fada ⑩

Grid Reference 15/205167 **WALK: MODERATE** 🚶🚶

Approximate Time: 1 hour 15 minutes
Distance: 4kms
How to get there: The quickest route leads from the east end of the Cam Loch, at **Grid Reference 15/234123**. Park off the A835 road near the bridge that crosses the Ledbeg River, and follow the track on foot out along the north side of Cam Loch. This path becomes less distinct as it meanders north towards Canisp, but follow the small cairns of stones placed periodically along the route. Soon the track becomes quite obvious again, and the loch, which is close to the path, comes into view. The 4km walk out is easy with no steep climbing and should take no more than 1 hr 15 minutes.

A long narrow strip of water, as the name depicts, just short of 1.5kms in length by a little less than 0.5kms at its widest, nestled at the southern base of Canisp, beside the hill footpath from Elphin to Lochinver via the Glencanisp Forest.

There are lots of nice, free taking, 8oz fish here, but also plenty of bigger trout to be had, making potential for some very good sport. Reports of trout in the 2-3lb classes are not infrequent but due to its location there is a lack of angling pressure so only a few reports are received each year. Bank fishing is easy all the way round and it's best in winds other than northerly as the mountain shelters it.

Looking out from Glas Bheinn across Assynt

22

Loch Veyatie ⑪

Grid Reference 15/180136

WALK: EASY 👣👣

Approximate Time:	n/a
Distance:	Roadside
How to get there:	Veyatie is long and narrow, running east to west for 6kms having an average width of around 400 metres.
Boat available:	Reach the waterside and the boat at **Grid Reference 15/209123**, by following the same directions as for Cam Loch, but actually drive down the road to where the boat is moored instead of parking at the gates. Make sure that the two gates en-route are re-locked after passing through. Information on where to obtain the gate keys will be given by the boat/permit vendor.

It is a big loch, and has a vast population of trout that vary in size considerably, along with shoals of arctic char. The char tend to stick to the deeper waters, but can sometimes be tempted to take a fly when feeding near the surface at any time of day. The brown trout here are of similar size to those in Cam Loch, although perhaps a little larger on average. Veyatie also hosts many fish in the 1-2½lb class but they are not easy to catch. The bigger specimens tend to take better in the late evening around dusk, given the right conditions, but occasionally one succumbs to a well presented fly during the day, so always watch out for something that pulls a lot harder than average and wants to make for the middle of the loch! Magnificent Mayfly hatches occur in June causing the trout to go into feeding frenzies both on the hatched adult surface fly and on the ascending nymph, so make sure there are some of those imitations in the box if fishing here at that time of year. The Mayfly also bring up lots of bigger fish that freely gorge on the feast as well, making this one of the best periods of the season to visit.

Bank fishing can sometimes produce very good baskets, but with few places to wade safely, wading is not generally necessary or recommended. Boat angling is the preferred method allowing a greater coverage of the water and giving access to all shorelines, which is particularly favourable if the wind should change direction. All the bays and hot spots can't be described here, but fishing in the shallower water, like elsewhere, brings the best results. If one place were to be singled out though it would be in the vicinity of the little rocky outcrops off the north shore and in the small reedy bay a little bit west of that area where the burn comes in from Loch Creagan Mor. Over the years, both places have produced more than their fair share of better fish. The loch is primarily weed free and deep with very few underwater hazards and consequently makes a first class water for trolling. Most years big ferox are taken here by this method with the largest in very recent times being a monster of 16½lbs, so specimen hunters should prospect here.

Veyatie is a particularly good evening and dusk venue, being the time that more of the larger fish come inshore to feed, and stories of very big fish crashing on flies and breaking leaders are not uncommon. Easterly or westerly winds make for good fishing and a brisk breeze, during daytime can often make it even better. Lying in a narrow east/west valley means that other wind directions tend to swirl creating difficult casting conditions for anglers.

On the safety theme, boating can be very dangerous in very strong easterly or westerly blows, so if in doubt err on the safe side and go ashore, even if the boat has to be left other than at the recognised anchorage.

Cam Loch ⑫

Grid Reference 15/210135   WALK: EASY 🚶🚶

Approximate Time:	15 minutes
Distance:	0.5kms
How to get there:	The boat is reached from the A835 road in the village of Elphin. Leave the highway near the old school and park out of the way near the very obvious two gates close by. Go through the unlocked gate and down the gravel road towards Loch Veyatie. After 200m or so take the rough trail off to the right for about 50m and then head down the hillside on a well-worn foot track to the wooden bridge over the River Abhainn Mor directly below.
Boat available:	Go over the bridge and follow the riverbank upstream for a few minutes where the boat and engine located at **Grid Reference 15/212124**, will be reached. From car to boat takes no longer than 15 minutes.

Camma is one of the larger lochs of Assynt covering an area of about 4kms in length by 1km at its widest. Made up of two distinct basins, the eastern one is relatively shallow and the western one very much deeper with a sub-surface gravel bank dividing the two at the loch's narrowest point. The eastern part is dotted with tree-covered islands with numerous underwater skerries between the western shore and the largest island Eilean na Gartaig, so do not attempt to use the outboard motor in this channel. The recommended route into the wider part of the eastern basin, and the only safe one under engine power, is via the narrow strait at the east end of Gartaig, which is a clear passageway. Fish around every islet, in all the bays, and right across this basin, where the trout are widespread and of good quality, but surface weed can be quite restrictive later in the season. It is well worth bank fishing from both the northern and southern shores and some good catches can be had by this means.

From Inchnadamph with Quinag in the distance

The deep western basin is a good trolling area for big ferox, but also some very good quality smaller trout can be found here mainly near the edges. It is effectively weed free but keep an eye open for the odd rocky protrusion when motoring close inshore. Cast your flies near the edges, across bays, and around headlands and pay particular attention to the cove at the western extremity, which can hold fish between 1 and 2lbs or more. During June, there are big hatches of Mayfly, which the trout feast on. This is when larger fish will come to the fly more readily and is an excellent time to visit.

The loch has a large population of hard fighting trout between 6-10ozs, including char, but now and again baskets will include some considerably bigger ones. As with many deep lochs a few really heavy fish are landed most seasons. The best in recent years taken whilst trolling, was a monster of 16lbs. Fish of 1-2lbs are not uncommon with the odd fish up to 5lbs being taken on fly occasionally. The loch fishes best in a southerly or westerly wind and for some reason does particularly well in high water conditions. Be careful though in strong easterly or westerly wind as big rolling waves can become dangerous making it unsafe for boating. Go ashore if in any doubt.

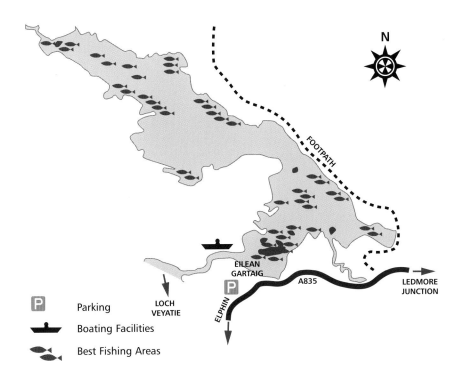

P Parking

Boating Facilities

Best Fishing Areas

Loch Ailsh

⑬

Grid Reference 15/315110   WALK: EASY 🚶🚶

Approximate Time:	n/a
Distance:	Roadside
How to get there:	Loch Ailsh is a sizeable water set in magnificent surroundings, at the top of the river Oykel. Access is gained by leaving the A837 road about 3kms east of the Altnacealgach Inn, and driving northeast along the rough road that leads to Benmore Lodge.
Boat available:	Some 2kms along this track the boat can easily be seen where it is moored at **Grid Reference 15/316103** and fishers should park close by where a short track leads to the anchorage. Do not drive any further than this point as the tarred route beyond is privately owned and maintained for the sole use of the residents and guests of Benmore Lodge.

Ailsh is a relatively shallow loch and best known for the run of salmon and sea trout that it gets later in the season. Don't however neglect the brown trout as they are of very good quality. Good numbers of fish up to 2lbs can be caught with the average, a hard fighting 12-14ozs. Ailsh fish can be fickle in their taking habits with lots of surface feeding for short spells, and then nothing until the next session begins but perseverance will get results. Fish can be caught anywhere, but round the edges, at the burn inflow, river outflow, and around the island are particularly good areas. The brown trout take best up to mid/end June and in westerly or southerly winds, but after that they become shy when the salmon and sea trout begin to turn up in good numbers.

Like all the trout fishing in the area there are no set bag limits but the loch is situated in the Kyle of Sutherland Conservation Area and so sensible restraint is requested when it comes to keeping one's catch. Fishing is from the boat only and no Sunday angling is allowed.

A lovely Ailsh trout comes to the net

Loch a Ghlinnen ①

Grid Reference 15/170234　　　**WALK: MODERATE** 🚶🚶

Approximate Time:	50 minutes
Distance:	2kms
How to get there:	Loch a Ghlinnen is en route to Loch Feith an Leothaid and so follow the same directions as laid out on page 28 of this booklet. The loch itself lies about 2kms from the road.
Boat available:	The boat is located at **Grid Reference 15/167234**. Allow 50 minutes or so to get there, and a bit less for the return journey.

A superb place to fish given the right day and conditions, Ghlinnen is home to a robust population of beautifully marked, hard fighting wild trout. The fact that they are very well shaped suggests that the feeding in this loch is excellent and their traditional red, black and golden markings make them a delight to catch. The fish vary in weight, up to and over 2lbs, but average more like 8-14ozs. Good baskets can be had here and at an altitude of 190 metres above sea level intrepid anglers are attracted by its solitude and scenic beauty in addition to its fishing potential. The trout are especially pink fleshed and are delicious to eat.

Ghlinnen produces good results from both bank and boat. There is no need for bank fishers to wade, as the loch is moderately deep around the edges. Good fish congregate later in the season off the burn mouth on the south east shore but don't miss out the bays around the outlet at the western end of the loch. A straight westerly or easterly wind is best as wind blowing from other any other quarter swirls all over the place and can test the fisher's patience!

A stunning 2lb 14oz trout from Loch a Ghlinnen

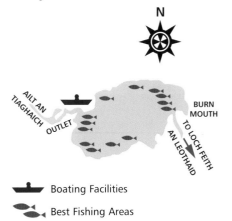

🚣 Boating Facilities

🐟 Best Fishing Areas

Loch Feith an Leothaid

2

Grid Reference 15/185225

WALK: TESTING 🚶🚶

Approximate Time:	1 hour 30 minutes
Distance:	3.5kms
How to get there:	To get there, start out from the lay-by beside the A837 road, about 400 metres east of the Keeper's Cottage at Little Assynt (**Grid Reference 15/157250**). Follow the path and cross the River Inver on the footbridge a short distance ahead. At this point the track turns right but do not follow it. Turn left and head east for about 50 metres, before making due south to the top of a little ridge just up in front. From here a view right across a wide area of moor (flattish land) is seen leading towards the gully that carries the Allt an Tiaghaich stream which flows from Loch a Ghlinnen. Traverse across this moorland towards the lower end of the gully. Once there, carry on up through the latter keeping to the east side of the stream until you reach Loch a Ghlinnen. Although simple enough with a well worn foot track from one end of the gully to the other, take care over the rocky outcrop half way up where a severe drop occurs down to the stream in the gorge below. Follow the burn in the north-east corner of the loch as it heads south-east further up the gully and Feith an Leothaid will be reached after a 20 minute walk.

A sizeable hill loch over 1km in length by over 0.5km in breadth, this place is full of table sized, usually free rising, fat, wild trout in a whole range of weights, with the average a bit less than the 8oz mark. Fair to say that specimen trout are unlikely to be caught here, but fine baskets of fighting fit trout are typical. Fish are caught all round the loch and this offers a wonderful day out in stunning scenery, with almost the expectation - but not the reality - of a fish at every cast. It is hence an excellent place for those new to fly-fishing for wild trout, and to other anglers who just desire to catch a few trout for their supper. The loch fishes well from the bank in most wind directions with little need for wading.

Follow the southern shoreline of Ghlinnen until you reach the large burn that comes in at the north east corner

of the loch and proceed upstream for about 1km which will bring you to Loch Feith an Leothaid. The distance from road to the loch is a little over 3kms, but as some of it is a little rough going, allow about 1.5 hours to get there with comfort.

Loch na Faoileige (The Gull Loch) ③

Grid Reference 15/213193　　　　　**WALK: TESTING** 🚶🚶

Approximate Time:	1 hour 30 minutes
Distance:	3.5kms
How to get there:	Like Loch na Beinne Reidhe just to the north, the walk in is generally uphill all the way over rough ground. The loch is located sitting on a fairly open area of rugged Highland moorland near the mountain's foot. Leave your car by the A837 road near or at Stronchrubie (**Grid Reference 15/247194**) and cross the Loanan River at a suitable point. Follow a line due west up the hill, picking out points to aim for along the way as it is easy to stray off course. Choose the best route over the rough and fairly steep ground to the top where it levels out somewhat as the loch is approached. It is approximately 3.5kms from the road taking the average person about 1.5 hours to get there.

Loch na Faoileige is tucked away on a plateau, at the northern base of Canisp, directly south from Loch na Beinne Reidhe mentioned just before. A small, high hill loch, at 450 metres above sea level it is set amongst dramatic scenery.

On a good day, a bag of quality fish can be taken from this water, averaging just under 1lb. The loch fishes well all round, but in the area of the islands at the east end, some better fish are sometimes seen. As with its northerly cousin mentioned above, the loch is sheltered, this time from the southwest by Canisp, another of Assynt's iconic mountains. It fishes well in any wind direction but it can be difficult in southwest when swirling air currents may cause serious disruption to an angler's casting technique!

If you have time, visit both Loch Dubh Meallan Mhurchaidh slightly to the north, and Loch nam Meallan Liatha further on again to the northwest. They are well populated with trout averaging around 6 to 8ozs, with a few bigger ones as well, particularly in Loch Dhubh Meallan Mhurchaidh. Usually the fish here are free rising, and offer great sport.

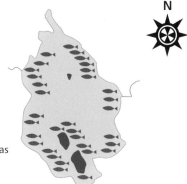

N

🐟 Best Fishing Areas

Loch na Beinne Reidhe

(4)

Grid Reference 15/213216

WALK: TESTING 𝅘𝅥𝅮𝅘𝅥𝅮

Approximate Time:	1 hour 30 minutes
Distance:	3.5kms
How to get there:	Park in the marked lay-by beside the A837 road about 800 metres south of the Inchnadamph Hotel. Cross over the River Loanan next to the road at a suitable point, as unfortunately, there is no bridge nearby, nor is there a path on the other side of the river. Pick a route and a point at the top of the hill in a westerly direction towards the loch and make for it, or better still check the map at this time and take a compass bearing. It is easy to stray off course as the surrounding landscape all looks pretty similar with few distinguishing features to assist in identifying the route. The loch sits in a small valley right at the top of the hill and only comes into view when close at hand. There are many 'false summits' en route to be aware of. The going is uphill over rough ground all the way and 1.5hrs should be allowed to cover the 3.5kms from the road to the water's edge.

A hill loch of note due to the quality and size of its trout. Set in a basin, 480 metres up, near the summit of Beinn Reidh, it stretches for about 1km in length by about 400 metres at its widest part.

Loch na Beinne Reidhe has a very good stock of trout, and the fact that only a few anglers will make the journey there each year helps to keep it that way. The fish are fat, typical in colour with big red and black spots and bright golden underbellies. They average around 1lb in weight but fish in the 2-3lb class have been caught here in the past, using standard fly patterns. As with other good lochs in the area the water is very clear which means stealth is the best weapon in the angler's armoury to avoid scaring the fish and sending them swimming into the deeps! The eastern shore is good, so work your flies carefully along it continuing round the headland on to the north bank. Some good fish have been taken where the loch narrows in the middle and in the bay opposite on the southern side. A major attraction to this loch is the fact that good baskets are possible given the right conditions, so a superb day's sport can be had on some occasions here. Most winds are good although anything from the southwest will create a flat calm or frustrating swirls, due to the surrounding topography. Bank fishing is easy with the potential to wade in some parts although this is not really necessary.

Looking down to an un-named loch

30

There is a smallish un-named loch nearby, just to the southwest of Ben Gharbh, at **Grid Reference 15/218220**. The fish here are large and plentiful, but lack girth. Best described as big and thin, and not so good for the table. Apparently they have always been like that, but nevertheless take freely and give great sport. It is well worth a cast or two on the way home.

Footnote

Bear in mind that the Loanan is a spate river, and if there is heavy rainfall during a visit to this loch, it may be dangerous or impossible to get back over the same crossing point later in the day.

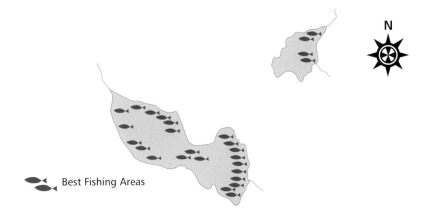

N

 Best Fishing Areas

A nice 2lb 11oz fish from Loch na Beinne Reidhe

Loch Culag (The School Loch) ⑤

Grid Reference 15/098216   **WALK: EASY** 🚶🚶

Approximate Time:	n/a
Distance:	Roadside
How to get there:	Access is very simply gained by taking the unclassified road south from Lochinver village at the Culag Bridge.
Boat available:	There is a small parking area denoted at the west side of the school enclosure fence to the north of the road and the boat is easily visible from there, being located at **Grid Reference 15/097218.**

About 500 metres from the ocean and 22 metres above it, the School Loch is irregularly shaped and covers an area of less than 20 hectares. It has a good population of hard fighting trout ranging from about 6ozs to 1lb, and is a very scenic spot, with the village school being located on a promontory in the loch. The Culag River, although not fishable itself, exits the loch near the school at the northwest corner, crashing rapidly to the Atlantic less than 1km away. Salmon and sea trout journey up the river to it from late June onwards, but whilst a good number remain, the majority carry on through the loch and the adjoining Glencanisp

River to settle in Loch Druim Suardalain, which is described on the following page 33. Being there at the right time in a west or southerly wind is the key to success on this water and although both southern arms become weed filled and un-fishable as the season progresses, there are still a lot of good clear areas available to fish.

Because of the local tradition and migratory fish present, no Sunday angling is allowed and only fishing from a boat is permitted with the same being located at **Grid Reference 15/097218.**

Loch Druim Suardalain (The Glen Loch) 6

Grid Reference 15/115218 **WALK: EASY**

Approximate Time: n/a
Distance: Roadside
How to get there: Heading south through the village of Lochinver, take the unclassified road on the left that leads to Glencanisp Lodge. A parking area is sited just over 1km from the village, and from here follow the rough track at the south side of the road to the footbridge at the outflow from the loch.
Boat available: Head east along the loch side until you reach the boat at **Grid Reference 15/109218**. The distance from road to the boat is about 500 metres.

Loch Druim Suardalain or the Glen Loch as it is locally known, lies about 1.5kms to the east of Lochinver village at the foot of Glencanisp. An especially attractive water, dotted with tree-covered islands, with the mountains of Canisp and Suilven rising to the east to form a spectacular background. Like its close neighbour Loch Culag, the Glen Loch has a good supply of eager brown trout ranging from small to maybe 1lb on a good day, but with salmon and sea trout arriving from July onwards there is always the chance, and quite a good chance if the conditions are right, of hooking something a bit bigger!

A west wind is first class here and best areas are around the islands, in the bay at the eastern end by the inflowing river, along the southern shoreline and at the western end of the loch in the vicinity of the out flowing stream. This place is all about having a nice relaxing day on an easily accessible and very attractive water set in stunning scenery with the chance of a salmon or sea trout later in the season. Neither Sunday or bank fishing is allowed.

Black-throated Diver chick

River Between Loch Gainimh & Loch Druim Suardalain ⑦

Grid Reference 15/170194 & 15/119218   **WALK: MODERATE** 🏃🏃

Approximate Time: n/a
Distance: River Length 6kms
How to get there: Initial access is as for Loch Druim Suardalain and simply continue from the car park on foot to Glencanisp Lodge, following the trail east that leads to the A835 road near Elphin. The river, for most of its length, is to the south side of the track, so choose your spot, fish and enjoy all that is around you.

This small spate river begins at the outflow from Loch Gainimh and ends its journey as it enters Loch Druim Suardalain. It is full of good sporting trout in all the common sizes with the odd bigger fish appearing when the conditions are right. Any amount of lovely pools, runs and lies, waterfalls and even mini lochs make up this stream as it meanders through a glen of outstanding natural beauty. It stretches for approximately 5kms and has two names, the first being Abhainn na Clach Airigh where it sets out from its source, and then somewhere midstream it changes to Abhainn bad na h-Achlaise for the remainder of its journey. The mountain of Canisp stands guard to the north, and Suilven takes care of the rest leaving the angler fishing amongst breathtaking surroundings.

There is a lot of walking as well as fishing on this trip, so be prepared for a good long day out in the hills. Some salmon and sea trout come through Loch Druim Suardalain later in the season inhabiting only the lower stretches of the river, below the first waterfall, which can make things increasingly interesting. Be aware that there is little point fishing here in drought conditions, so check water heights and weather forecasts before setting out and be rewarded accordingly.

The river between Loch Gainimh and Loch Druim Suardalain with Suilven in the background

Approximate Time:	2 hours
Distance:	7kms
How to get there:	Take the footpath east from Glencanisp Lodge for about 5kms until you reach the point (**Grid Reference 15/167197**) that lies midway between the two marked footbridges. Leave the path here and head south west towards Suilven aiming for Loch a Choire Dhuibh. The route here suffers badly from foot erosion caused by the vast numbers of walkers trekking towards the peak. Once at Loch a Choire Dhuibh, progress on to all of the others in the chain for a great day out. The walk in is a little over 7kms, but because of the rough hill climb over the last section, make sure to allow a good two hours for the trip.

This small hill loch is to be found at the northwestern end of Suilven, Assynt's most iconic and majestic Mountain. It sits around 300 metres above sea level and harbours a good stock of free rising fish averaging somewhere in the 4-8oz bracket. Nice baskets are easily caught here in most wind directions with the hill sheltering the loch from the south side. Barrack is surrounded by a good number of other small tarns, which generally host similar sized trout. This is an excellent place to wander for a day amongst the myriad of small waters where just about every step taken in any direction leads to another loch full of golden, hard fighting little brownies, only visited by a handful of anglers each season if that.

These tarns were known locally and collectively as one of the better places to fish, with the old gamekeepers making at least one sojourn up there each year. Keepers generally did not go to such places unless the fishing was good, and with the chance of a much better fish, so be sure to cover even the smallest of waters just in case that is

where those bigger fish were then, or still are now! Barrack and its immediate neighbour, Loch a Choire Dhuibh, are more or less weed clear, but some of the other smaller ones have surface growth all over. This is truly a wild, arresting area to fish, where the variety of waters makes for both a dynamic and especially interesting day.

It does take a while to get there but the walk in is magnificent and is easily argued to be justification alone for making the trip.

A cracking 5lb 6oz trout from Assynt

Approximate Time:	1 hour
Distance:	5kms
How to get there:	To gain access to Fionn, transport should be left in the public parking area by the unclassified coastal road from Lochinver, about one kilometre or thereby, south of Inverkirkaig Village, near the road bridge over the River Kirkaig. Go through the 'kissing gate' and up the road ahead for about two hundred metres. Here the footpath for Suilven and Fionn Loch branches off to the right. Follow the track, which undulates and meanders through the Kirkaig Valley, until reaching the loch, some three and a half kilometres ahead. Take time to enjoy this journey, which is a really scenic route, passing the spectacular 'Falls of Kirkaig' on the way. The loch will be located in about one hour.
Boat available:	The boat is found at **Grid Reference 15/123178**, and an outboard motor is also stored there.

Fionn is often described by locals as one of the 'best lochs' in Assynt. It sits 109 metres above sea level and stretches lazily along the southern base of Suilven in spectacular surroundings with Cul Mor to the east and Stack Pollaidh to the south. It is 3.5km long by 600 metres at its widest and holds a superb head of brown trout and arctic char.

The loch is divided into three distinct sections, western, middle and eastern, each being separated from the other by shallow and narrow areas. Fionn fishes very well from a boat as the common westerly breeze makes for long drifts that skirt the edges of the enticing bays on each shoreline requiring only minor adjustments to keep in line. The boat also allows easy access to the lesser fished north shore which otherwise requires a lengthy walk round the loch's western end. This being said, bank fishing can be just as good and in some areas wading gives an advantage.

The western and middle sections of the loch tend to be deeper and weed free

with the small bays being the most productive areas. In addition whilst brownies are the main quarry some anglers troll successfully for large ferox trout that inhabit the depths of the western and middle sections. This water is fishable in most winds with west or east being favourable.

The eastern section is slightly elevated creating a stream in the narrows where it joins the middle section. It is comparatively shallow with patchy weed growth throughout, and the bed undulates from gentle shallow banks to deeper areas providing very attractive lies. Lots of smaller fish live here and give fine sport but there are plenty of bigger specimens too, and each season a number of fish between 1 and 2lbs are caught from this location.

A spectacular channel some 60 metres wide makes up the last section to the eastern extremity where it meets the in-flow from Loch Veyatie.

Fionn Loch in the foreground with Loch Sionascaig in the distance

This particularly good part is home to large numbers of beautiful trout in diverse sizes, and in high water conditions becomes river like with a very definite flow running throughout its length. The area around the Veyatie inflow has also produced some cracking fish of up to 3lbs in recent years and is always well worth the effort of getting there.

Fionn is enigmatic and scenically one of the finest places to fish in the area. Hosting a big head of trout around the 8oz mark that are of excellent fighting quality, pink fleshed and delicious eating. It also has a fair number of splendid fish in the 1-2lb bracket, ultimately offering a very real chance of landing the fish of a lifetime!

A lone 'float tuber' has reported hooking, seeing and subsequently losing two big fish on the same day. One estimated in excess of 5lbs and the other around 10lbs! Both fish broke the angler's leader and were encountered in the western end of the middle section.

PATH

INVER KIRKAIG

RIVER KIRKAIG

FOOTPATH

N

Boating Facilities

Best Fishing Areas

LOCH VEYATIE

Un-named Loch at base of Suilven ⑩

Grid Reference 15/140187 WALK: TESTING 🚶🚶

Approximate Time:	2 hours
Distance:	6kms
How to get there:	To get to there, follow exactly the same directions as for Fionn Loch. About 0.5km from the latter, the path divides and a cairn of stones marks this spot. Turn left here and continue on the track, round the west end of Fionn Loch into Coire Mor. When about the middle of the corrie, leave the path, keeping to the right of the stream and head northeast up the steep hillside ahead until the plateau is reached. Continue northeast over the flatter terrain to the loch which only comes into view during the last few hundred metres on approach. The whole journey, which is a bit more than 6kms, takes about 2 hours to complete, and a little less on the way back.

Another very good little loch situated near the western end of Suilven about 260 metres above sea level. Seldom fished because of its inaccessibility, it holds quite a number of large, deep-bodied trout of superb quality. An average fish here would be well over 1lb in weight but little inhibits their growth and so a good number of fish up to and over 3lbs are also found in this tarn. Not easy to catch, so blank days are common, despite the fact that big trout are usually seen cruising on the surface and near the shore when feeding. This tarn lies on a plateau right at the base of the mountain, and is exposed to winds from all quarters, the best for fishing being from the south, which makes for easy casting along both sides of the loch. Fish with confidence all round, and as with other small waters, cast carefully so as not to scare the fish that often lie close inshore.

Remember the conservation aspect of these small wild waters so please help them continue into the future by sensibly limiting the number of fish that you keep, if any.

Un-named loch at the base of Suilven

Uidh Fhearna River
between Loch Veyatie and Fionn Loch ⑪

Grid Reference 15/150158   WALK: MODERATE 👫

Approximate Time:	1 hour 30 minutes
Distance:	6kms
How to get there:	To gain access, either hire the boat on Veyatie (page 23) and motor down, or hire the boat on Fionn (page 36) and motor up there. Follow the directions already given for getting to those lochs, and proceed.

A broad river flowing from Loch Veyatie into Fionn Loch, measuring just over 1km in length by about 40 metres wide in places. It is well worth the effort, but only during periods of high water. There are lots of fish in this river and many small ones too, but coupled with good numbers in the 1lb region and some larger ones as well, it is a great place to cast a fly. Either a fish caught, or some sort of action with every cast is not unusual, giving tremendous fun on the day for anyone making the effort to get there. Wading is almost essential to obtain the best sport, although there are one or two places where it can be fished easily from the bank. As with any river like this, it is only really worth fishing when a good amount of water is present, providing a high oxygen level for the trout and a steady stream of food coming down in the heightened flow. Just west of Veyatie the river transforms into a small loch several hundred yards long, prior to gliding, tumbling and rushing through several pools, runs and lies, before finally cascading into Fionn. Although relatively short, this river provides oodles of angling, so fish every yard, as it all holds a great stock of eager, hard fighting, trout.

One angler who recently spent seven days fishing for salmon in Russia, said that he enjoyed his few hours on this river better than his whole week over there!

Attractive water on the river near Loch Veyatie

Loch a Choin (The Dog Loch) ⑫

Grid Reference 15/084186   **WALK: EASY** 🚶🚶

Approximate Time:	5 minutes
Distance:	500 metres
How to get there:	To get to the 'Dog' from Lochinver, take the unclassified coastal route south. Cross the road bridge over the River Kirkaig beyond Inverkirkaig village, and continue for another kilometre to the first roadside loch. Leave the car in the small tarred parking area near the south west corner of this tarn. Come back along the road for about 200 metres and head southeast up the hillside where a well worn foot track leads to the loch 5 minutes walk away.
Boat available:	The boat is located at **Grid Reference 15/082187**.

This small loch is best fished from the boat with bank angling not possible along its tree clad southwestern shore. Wading is not possible anywhere as the water is too deep at the edges for this activity although in general the loch is relatively shallow. The whole loch can be well covered from the boat with only a small section of weed growth at the eastern extremity. A water which is very sheltered from most winds but northwest and southeast ones catch it well and it fishes best in those conditions.

The trout population here is not high, but the inhabitants are of excellent quality. Although never easy to tempt in the gin clear water, they grow in excess of 2½lbs with much bigger fish undoubtedly in residence. Although not big enough to spend a whole day on, it is well worth fishing in the right circumstances and can be combined with its neighbour, Loch an Arbhair (the Cat Loch), to make a good outing of it. This second loch is back by the

roadside and holds a good stock of common sized trout, which can be fished for, from either the boat or bank with boat being the preferred option. The vessel's location here is at **Grid Reference 15/078187**.